AN HONEST CHANCE

AN HONEST CHANCE

HOW TO GIVE A PROBLEM EMPLOYEE AN HONEST CHANCE TO IMPROVE OR LEAVE IN FIVE STRESS-FREE STEPS

Marvin Franklin

Writers Club Press

San Jose   New York   Lincoln   Shanghai

An Honest Chance
How to Give a Problem Employee AN HONEST CHANCE To Improve or
Leave in Five Stress-Free Steps

Writers Club Press
an imprint of iUniverse, Inc.

For information address:
iUniverse, Inc.
5220 S. 16th St., Suite 200
Lincoln, NE 68512
www.iuniverse.com

This is in part a work of fiction but inspired by actual events. The reader will
recognize reality in the types of situations presented in the case studies,
however the names of persons, places, and companies are inventions of the
author. Any resemblance to people living or deceased is purely coincidental.

ISBN: 0-595-22142-4

Printed in the United States of America

Contents

Foreword

Variety is the spice of life, and so it can also be with simplicity. Every now and then we find that a problem is solved by something so simple, so natural, that we feel it has been familiar to us our entire life. That is the comfortable way managers react when reading about the Five Phases of working with problem employees. Suddenly, problem employees no longer exist. They will either adjust and become productive or they will leave your employment—all without undue stress.

Sooner or later, almost every manager has at least one troublesome employee—someone who can undermine the organization's effectiveness and perhaps the manager's own career. The Five Phases of handling such employees, once learned, will guide every step in achieving ideal results.

Easy to visualize, the Five Phases have been used successfully by thousands of managers. Most managers perform the first two phases without even thinking about them. Phase 1 is called "HELP" and Phase 2 is also called "HELP." Because most managers already spend too much time "helping," the focus of this book is on what to do next. Readers will be encouraged not to stay in a HELP phase so long that they become frustrated or, worse yet, that their other employees become frustrated—irritated that their manager doesn't take more timely corrective action. Giving "help" is definitely encouraged but, as experienced managers know, too much "help" for one individual can reduce overall productivity and weaken the manager's team.

There are only three other phases. When managers identify which Phase they are in, they will confidently and comfortably proceed to the next step. They will have "Five-Phase Awareness." They will enjoy managing more than they did before. The Five Phase approach offers an additional bonus, that of helping to keep good employees–ones that were just thought to be problem employees.

Introduction

Perhaps you have a problem employee who is driving you nuts, or perhaps you feel guilty because you've kept the non-performer around. If it has persisted that long, your suffering can soon be over. Never again will you let an employee problem linger to the extreme, because now you'll be comfortably prepared in advance for every situation.

You've been the best manager you can be. You've probably read *The One Minute Manager* and books on psychology and management. You've tried everything with your "problem employee," your "PE," as we'll call them here. By not firing the "PE" outright, you have shown that you have a conscience. (Or perhaps you're afraid of the legal ramifications, or afraid of the employee, or of the company's Human Resources Manager. If you own the company you might be concerned about appearing too harsh or too foolish. Or perhaps you're just apprehensive or you simply haven't thought about what to do next.)

It's easy to feel all alone in searching for an answer. It may be because your own manager is avoiding the problem or is testing you, or doesn't seem to care as long as your group is still productive. Perhaps your manager will only commiserate with you. Some managers–even very senior ones–try to avoid employee issues because they are uncomfortable themselves with the solutions and are too familiar with the career-threatening risks of inappropriate handling. They may feel that they don't know the problem employee well enough to make a recommendation. No one wants to be identified with bungling a personnel problem. "PE's" can mean big trouble. After all, their first name is "Problem."

So, there you are, knowing that something has to be done. Your leadership may even be in question. You feel the stress. If you don't act soon, the people that have been making you look so good may decide that you're not the person they want to work for. And what's a manager worth without capable people?

You know that a skilled manager is one who establishes the right environment for his people to be productive. This book will help you maintain a pleasant and productive environment for all of your employees–even the ones that are having trouble, and, as we'll find, some of those are not truly "PE's."

They will all benefit from an honest chance.

Chapter 1

Selecting an Assassin

Ed Gannon's career had accelerated so rapidly that he felt blessed with enormous luck. There was no hint that his upward momentum might not continue.

His parents had raised him well, their primary demands being to do his best, respect others, and serve his country. His best had led to an appointment at the Air Force Academy, where he was captain of the basketball team, and then into combat flying, where he further distinguished himself. After four years of active duty, he resigned to become a test pilot for a company building military aircraft. His ideas led to the design of a new ejection seat for a troublesome fighter, the X-127, that had already lost too many pilots. For his accomplishments, Ed was introduced to Julius Redding, the very thankful Chief Executive Officer of his company.

Redding took a liking to young Gannon and transferred him to the division headquarters where fighter planes were designed and built. It turned out to be one of Julius's many brilliant moves as an industry leader. Quickly, one success followed another, and Ed was repeatedly promoted. Soon, there was no higher to go unless Julius brought him to the corporate staff. Ed became a Group Vice President at age 36.

*   *   *

The story that follows is true with the names and descriptions of people and organizations altered to protect those involved. It's hard to believe that it happened in one of the largest companies in the world and that it was the Chief Executive Officer who conceived the plot. Every reader will solve this problem better than Julius Redding.

Julius, 62 years old, having inherited his position from the firm's founder, a fellow aviation pioneer, ruled "Aerospace Giant" with an iron fist. Although an autocrat, Julius was well respected by his employees and others in the industry. He was a rarity–one of the early barnstorming pilots still in a major position of authority. He was a natural leader and an excellent judge of talent. His white hair, broad smile, and crusty manner in addressing issues, were familiar to workers throughout the organization. However, unseen by others, except for those who were closest to him in the executive offices, Julius had a nagging problem which had haunted him for many months without resolution. That ubiquitous issue was soon to effect the rest of Ed Gannon's life.

Ed's appointment to headquarters a month earlier, had not been an entirely favorable experience. He had liked the creativeness involved in division operations and there had been a true sense of camaraderie that he had thought was present throughout Julius's empire. To his surprise, he did not see the same positive interaction between the executives on the corporate staff. There seemed a certain uneasiness, a tightness.

This particular day had started off well, but it would end badly. Julius had invited him to an early breakfast in the executive dining room before the others arrived. Julius had been cheerful, telling stories of missing high school, how being short in stature had helped him become a pilot, his early days in flying, and his future plans for the company.

Later, they walked down the old-fashioned mahogany-paneled corridor of the executive suite with Julius's hand resting on Ed's much higher shoulder. Suddenly, Julius saw his old friend, the Vice Chairman of The Board, Walt Bramlett, pop out of an office and start down the hall in front of them. Julius lowered his eyes and slowed Ed up so as not to attract Walt's attention. After a moment, the older man said, "Let's do some talking in my office." Julius's face had completely sobered.

*　　　　　*　　　　　*

On the way, Julius thought about Walt Bramlett. Something had to be done. Walt was the same age as Julius. They had grown up flying together, often competing, but always companions, always buddies. Ten years ago, Walt had been the closest rival for Chairman and CEO, but the Board of Directors had given the nod to Julius. For eight years they continued to be friends. For eight years Julius listened to Walt's ideas and valued them.

It wasn't clear to outsiders just when things started to change, but Julius knew. Walt kept sticking his nose into matters concerning profit and loss and the new Vice President of Finance didn't appreciate Walt's prying. Julius had given Walt some good-natured hints to back off, but Walt, in his take-charge manner, and concerned about the changing financial policies, had continued his intrusions.

Julius and Walt had always argued. It brought out the best in each of them. But soon, not knowing how to control Walt's behavior, Julius became uncomfortable. He began avoiding Walt's opinions. Even though they worked only a few offices apart, they rarely spoke. An uneasy two years passed—awkward for them and extremely awkward for the rest of the executives on mahogany row.

When they came to his office, Julius ushered Ed in and motioned for him to take one of the heavy leather chairs. Julius stiffly sat down behind his own over-sized desk. It was a large office by any standards, but the furniture wasn't as refined as today's. Even though the company produced modern jet fighters, the decor spoke more of a nostalgic era in early aviation.

By the arrangement it was clear to anyone entering the room that the man behind the desk was in charge, and if you were sitting low in one of the heavy leather chairs, looking up at Julius Redding, it was especially clear who was in charge.

Since seeing Walt Bramlett in the hall, the pleasant atmosphere had evaporated. Ed sat silently waiting for Julius to speak.

The CEO eyed a model plane on his desk. It was one of the single engine World War II fighters the company had mass produced. He traced his finger over the body. He touched the propeller so that it barely turned. "Ed, I have something for you to do."

"Of course, anything you say."

Julius leaned back in his chair, where he seemed less commanding. He closed his eyes, then pursed his lips, and turned his chair toward the window. "Ed, you know Walt Bramlett."

"Yes, sir, before coming here, at an industry association meeting where he was speaking. And, of course, he's come to the division a number of times to help us out with designs."

Julius turned to stare at Ed, "I know you know him. You'd have to be brain dead to be in this business and not know Walt. And I know he's a design genius. Always has been. Intuitive. No education for it, either." He paused, closing his eyes again. "But you don't know Walt as closely as others on the staff."

"No, sir. I'm sure of that."

"You're the right man, Ed." Julius's eyes remained closed, his forehead deeply furrowed. The silence lengthened. His hand reached out to touch the desk as though to support himself. "Tell Walt we want him to resign."

Ed's eyes opened wide, looking for a sign from Julius that he might be kidding.

"Well, can you handle it?"

"I can handle whatever you say, sir. I just didn't expect…" He didn't finish the sentence.

"Okay, then. Get it done. Today or tomorrow. Let me know, but keep me out of it." Julius still had his eyes closed. "That's all now." He opened his eyes and reached over to the model plane, giving the propeller a rapid spin. When it stopped, he turned towards Ed, staring at him. "That's all."

Chapter 2

The Hit Man

On reaching his own office, Ed called Walt's secretary and made an appointment for the next day, then leaned uneasily back in his chair to think of what he would say. He was committed to the mission.

Why had Julius given him this filthy job? Ed wasn't born when the two buddies had been skimming tree tops in their bi-planes. Perhaps, Bramlett was expecting the message.

That night, Ed struggled to sleep as he searched for the best way to carry out his assignment. After reminding himself that it might not be a surprise, he finally dozed off.

At exactly 10:00 a.m. Ed arrived outside Walt's office and was warmly greeted. The secretary brought in a silver tray with English China and a pot of obligatory coffee which she placed on the low teakwood table between the two men. Ed took a sip, relishing the warmth, and appreciating the delay.

"What brings the newest Group Vice President to this out-of-the-way office?" asked the older man, placing his cup on a saucer, which made the familiar click of fine china.

"Yes, sir. Julius sent me," said Ed, looking for a sign from Walt that he knew what was coming.

Unfortunately, there was no sign, only silence.

"Are you waiting for me to guess the purpose?" asked Bramlett with a trace of a frown on his brow.

"No sir, not at all, sir. Sorry..."

"For a Vice President, you're having difficulty in coming to the point. You seemed more comfortable running your division. Tell me why Julius asked you to come."

Ed looked up into the friendly eyes of a man with the furled leather skin of an outdoors man, a hearty but easy-going person who was invariably polite.

Walt Bramlett's eyes began to narrow as he observed Ed. "Speak up," he said gently.

"Yes, sir. I have a message to deliver." Ed paused as he continued to search Bramlett's face, then he spoke, using Julius's words, "We want you to resign." Ed watched as the friendly eyes turned into questioning ones and then froze, as Bramlett struggled to digest the message.

When Bramlett finally spoke his voice remained soft but now it carried an edge, "Are you telling me I'm fired? Is Julius sending our newest executive to tell me that?"

"Not fired, sir. It's a retirement."

"Don't insult me, Mr. Gannon, I don't have to listen to hog-wash. You and I are done. Julius will have to explain this." Bramlett stood up.

"Look," said Ed, rising from his chair, "if Julius had felt up to seeing you, don't you think he would have?"

Bramlett glared at him.

"You're friends, Mr. Bramlett, he couldn't see you."

In the next hour, Ed repeated those same words many times as Walt Bramlett vacillated between rage, confusion, and tear-filled silence. Bramlett didn't understand why he had been ignored the last two years, and he wasn't finding out now. His shoulders were stooped when he finally said good-bye to Ed, then walked to his desk and sat down, staring out the window. One of the company's latest jet fighters flashed across the runway. He had flown every model the company had ever produced.

Ed walked down the hall, past the row of secretaries, to his own office. He dialed Redding. The secretary put him through. "Julius, I told Walt. He won't be coming to see you."

"Thanks, Ed. Good work." The receiver went down.

That was it. Ed leaned over his desk, exhausted. He didn't want to think about it. He absentmindedly threw a few papers in his briefcase. He straightened out some pictures. He was working for an aviation hero, a legend, a......He wondered how in the future he could protect himself from Julius. How do you do that when the man doesn't talk to you if he has a problem?

Ed vowed never again to be the foil, never again to be Julius's hit man, and to start looking for employment elsewhere.

*   *   *

That day, Julius Redding left work early with the intention of stopping at The Proudest Penguin, a favorite watering hole where patrons could watch commercial liners coming in to land. He told himself that he had stepped up to a very difficult task, that of letting an old friend go. What more could be expected of an executive? Anyone could understand his not being able to face his friend at such a time. They had been inseparable. Walt had been responsible for much of Julius's own success. Certainly Walt would understand. He just didn't fit on the team any more. No one from the inner circle could have told Walt; it had to be someone else and Ed Gannon, a newcomer, had been the perfect answer. Walt wouldn't like the decision but he would respect it. Ed wouldn't understand the decision but he'd admire the humane way of delivering such a message.

When Julius approached The Proudest Penguin, he realized that Walt might also be going there. Besides, there were too many memories. Julius decided to go directly home.

*   *   *

Minutes later, a shaky Walt Bramlett drove slowly away from his office. He found it difficult to focus on the road. He couldn't grasp what had happened. One day he was on the inside of the huddle helping to call the plays, then he was on the outside looking in, and finally he hadn't even known where the huddles were taking place or what plays had already been called. He had been given ceremonial duties and kept at a distance.

What had the problem been? Was he supposed to know? If he'd known would he have been able to do anything about it? The questions would go unanswered.

On Thursdays, Walt regularly stopped at The Proudest Penguin, but this evening he didn't want to face the crowd. He drove on.

*　　　　　*　　　　　*

Julius never again visited The Proudest Penguin, nor did Walt.

*　　　　　*　　　　　*

Eight years later, Julius attended a magnificent farewell party given in his honor. The most prominent people in the industry came from every modern country, along with celebrities from Hollywood and the nation's capital. Speeches were given to his greatness and his contributions to aviation.

Ed Gannon was not in attendance. He had long since found a lesser paying job at another firm. Nobody missed him. Aerospace Giant was far too large to miss one young vice president.

Neither did Walt Bramlett attend the party. For a few years he had tried a career as a consultant but tired of the excessive travel. He wanted to spend more time with his wife. Then, she had died. Two years ago, on a beautiful clear day, he had flown a small plane out of the Santa Barbara Airport and headed over the mountains to the San Joaquin Valley. The wreckage was found forty miles west of Bakersfield, augured into the ground in the geometric center of a vineyard, far from any dwelling. There wasn't enough left of the craft, or of Walt, to discover what might have gone wrong.

*   *   *

When Ed Gannon had read in the papers of Walt's crash, he left work and drove to Santa Monica Beach. He walked across the sand and sat down far from the waves. He knew that even if Walt's engine had failed, the plane was capable of gliding miles to a soft landing. He thought of the spinning propellor on Julius's desk. Before he left, the water was lapping at his feet. The sun had fallen below the horizon.

Chapter 3

Reconstructing The Crime

Ed had never mentioned to anyone his role in Walt's dismissal, nor, out of loyalty, had he told of Julius's behavior. Instead of grousing, Ed had found other work and more recently, twenty years following the incident, had joined *Upscale Jets*, as Executive Vice President and Chief Operating Officer.

After a year, Ed was already being considered for President. A three man search committee had been appointed by the board of directors. One other man within *Upscale Jets*, the VP of International Operations, was also being considered.

The search committee had a high regard for Ed's integrity and for what he had apparently accomplished in his first year. However, it was always difficult to determine within such a short span of time, whether the successes were due to good management, good luck, or the inherited momentum of the predecessor.

Ed was criticized by some for how he spent part of his time. There was an insistent, sniping rumor that the hours he devoted to personally conducting Management Development classes was not appropriate for an Executive Vice President. A friend said that it was the VP of International, his opponent, who had started the attacks.

Teaching in the management classes had started within four months of his joining Upscale Jets. Ed had approached the Vice President of Human Resources and made his offer. He wanted to personally coach his managers on how problem employees should be handled, including how they should be worked with before they became problem employees, so that they might never become "PE's." Ed developed a Five Phase approach and taught it with an earnest manner that left noone in doubt that he believed in it and knew from experience that it worked.

He used stories to illustrate his methods and one of them was of Julius Redding and the firing of Walt Bramlett. He meticulously disguised the names and identities of the real characters, including himself.

Now, standing in front of the classroom, Ed faced the 24 managers in the current class who had just heard him tell the tragedy of Redding and Bramlett. One of the third-level managers attending was Maria Parker, the niece of Robert Parker, a member of the Board of Directors who was serving as Chairman of the Search Committee for a new president. Maria was in her early thirties and had risen rapidly because of her talent–not because of her uncle. She wore a dark blue baseball cap with the company's logo embroidered on it in thick gold threads.

"It really happened that way," said Ed, "You've heard basic descriptions of the Five Phases. Walt Bramlett was in trouble with his boss."

Ed knew they didn't understand the Five Phases well enough yet, but he asked the question anyway, "What Phase was he in when the young corporate VP called on him?"

He pointed at the flip chart in front of the class, where the Five Phases were listed.

*   *   *   *   *   *   *

1. Help
2. Help
3. Show concern. Discuss it.
4. Show serious concern. Discuss it.
5. Probation

*   *   *   *   *   *   *

The managers pondered in silence.

"It's imperative to know," said Ed, "what Phase you're in. Then you'll know how to proceed. Everyone will want to develop Five-Phase Awareness."

One of the younger managers, Angus Cassidy, finally spoke up in his Irish brogue, "The mon musta been on probation."

"But probation is always done in writing," said Ed, "and Walt Bramlett didn't know why he was an outcast."

"Wull, I thought that maybe big executives didn't necessarily do things by the book."

"True," said Ed, "but they should. It would be easier on them."

Again, there was silence.

"Okay," said Ed, "I understand your uncertainty. The words on the chart don't tell you enough, but after this session and reading the notes I'll give you, you'll understand. Let's discuss each of the Phases and then decide which Phase Walt was in. I'm going to go rapid fire." Ed grabbed a pointer, aimed it at the first phase, and began:

"**Phase 1.** 'Help'. You see an employee having trouble with their work. You offer help because that's the natural thing to do. You show them how, or why, or whatever else it takes. Perhaps you'll have someone else help them. The main thing is to get the job done. Right?" asked Ed.

The class nodded.

Ed noticed Maria Parker sitting in the front row with her arms crossed. He knew Maria could influence her uncle, especially whether Ed's classroom time was productive.

"**Phase 2,**" said Ed, "'Help'. Same story. Just because a little help didn't work, you probably won't give up. Phase 2 is merely to emphasize that the manager's primary responsibility is to get the job done, and that most often means giving help."

Angus Cassidy tossed his head back and grinned. "Walt Bramlett must not 'ave been in Phase 1 or 2," he said, "because the only 'elp 'e got was being 'elped out the door."

The class nervously chuckled.

Ed smiled and continued. "Perhaps Julius thought he had already given Walt as much help as he could. But if that was the case, why didn't Walt know what the problem was?"

Ed looked at Maria Parker and smiled. "Is your body language any indication of your thinking?"

Maria immediately sat more erect and unfolded her arms. "People aren't that open with each other," she said.

"I know," said Ed, "if they were we wouldn't have to take time to talk about it–why it's better to be more open. That's part of what this session is about. I'll try to convince you by showing how much easier it is for everyone."

Maria slowly nodded.

"Willing to keep an open mind until I'm done?" asked Ed.

She smiled. It was a cautious smile, but attractive.

"We have a skeptic," said Ed. "That'll keep us on our toes. Let's go on." He returned to his fast pace.

"**Phase 3**. 'Show Concern. Discuss it'. The third Phase is simply the point at which the manager realizes that he has given all the help he can, or all the help that seems reasonable, and yet the employee is not responding sufficiently. When you first come to that realization, it's time to 'Show Concern, and Discuss it'. That means having a frank discussion with the employee–what people used to call a 'Dutch Uncle Talk'.

"Notice that this Phase isn't called just 'Show Concern'. That's because some people think they can show concern by how they wiggle their body, or by snide remarks, or by jokes, or by hints. Maybe they can, but too many times the employee doesn't get the right message. Walt Bramlett didn't. That's why it needs to be discussed. It's called 'Show Concern. Discuss it'.

"Before having the 'Dutch Uncle Talk' ask yourself if you've done everything reasonable to help. Have you made it clear what is expected? Have you given sufficient coaching? Have you assigned others to help in training or coaching?

"But, don't exhaust yourself searching for what might be done, because the next step with the employee will not be that serious. It's a simple discussion that avoids threats. The conversation could be as light as asking, 'Say, Sam, you've been here a month now and your weekly reports keep coming in late. Is there any doubt in your mind that they have to be in by 4:00 p.m. Fridays? It's causing me trouble. I've got to have them in on time.'

"Sam can respond in different ways.

"Number one possibility: He might be embarrassed and say he didn't know how important it really was, and that he won't let it happen again. If Sam responds that way, the problem is most likely solved. You didn't threaten. You maintained a professional and friendly relationship. And Sam doesn't look like he's going to become a PE.

"Number two possibility: If Sam offers a rash of question-able excuses, you may have a sizeable problem. If some of the excuses are valid, you might be lenient and let Sam off the hook by offering suggestions and ending with, 'Sam, you do know that the reports have to be on time and that it's impor-tant?' There is no hint of a threat. For a Phase 3 conversation you should avoid threats."

A voice from the back questioned him, "But what if the guy has a bad attitude?"

"You probably know in advance what to expect," said Ed, slowing up from his torrid pace, "but a Dutch Uncle talk can bring out surprises. If you find a negative attitude, you might introduce just a hint of a threat. Listen to what it sounds like if I add just a few words to what I said before: 'Sam, you do know that the reports have to be on time and that it's impor-tant *to your job performance?*'

"That's a meaningful addition. If you feel it's necessary, you say it."

Maria Parker raised her hand. "Is that actually going past Phase 3?"

"It might be," said Ed, "but just a tiny step. It's not yet Phase 4. Sometimes a Phase 3 conversation can roll over into a Phase 4. You want to avoid that, and in the above situation I initially did avoid it. Later, because of the employee's attitude, I moved toward Phase 4 in order to still be honest.

"Sometimes–not very often–you have to go even further. I'd like to say 'never' go further, but sometimes you just have to glide right into a full Phase 4 conversation. That has some risks which we'll discuss later.

"Time to move on.

"**Phase 4** is called 'Show serious concern. Discuss it'. For example, it might begin with something like: 'Sam, your reports are still coming in late. I'm seriously concerned about your performance and your attitude. Your excuses aren't helping. If the work continues to be late, your job will be in jeopardy. You'll be on probation or out of work. This is important. Do you think you can correct it?'"

Ed opened his hands to the class. "Not too tough to do, right? That's because I didn't wait until I was so frustrated with the employee that I became angry, or abusive. And notice, I used the word 'serious'."

Maria asked, "What if Sam says he doesn't think he can do it?"

"That's where honest conversation pays off," said Ed. "Your next question to Sam might be, 'Then, you're giving up? What do you propose? Are you going to resign? If not, do you prefer going into probation?'

"Or perhaps you think Sam has talent for some other position, in which case you might ask, 'Sam, do you think you'd like to be in a customer support job? Something that doesn't require report writing?'"

"That'll bring it to a 'ead," said Angus.

"Yes," said Ed, "and it could likely work smoothly from that point forward. If you need the employee's cooperation in the transition of his work, you will probably have it."

Angus raised his hand. "Why the big deal about delay between Phase 3 and 4?"

"Okay, we may as well answer that now. There are two factors to consider. Remember, that you enter Phase 3 when you *first* realize–after all the help you've given–that you are not getting sufficient results. That means you can enter Phase 3 at any time. You don't need to consult with your own manager or with Human Resources. You're just communicating. If you start too early to think about warnings, you'll get off on the wrong foot. Your goal is to get results and you are assuming that a discussion will help. That's the first factor to consider.

"The second factor is this: Before you get into a Phase 4 conversation, you want to be well prepared. The employee will most likely feel threatened. You want to go about it in such a way that the employee will have the best chance to come out of it successfully. That's good for both of you, and certainly the company. But you have to be ready for how the employee may respond to you. You may end up telling them that they are going to be put on probation or worse.

"For that, in most companies, and certainly in this company, you need the advance approval of your management and Human Resources. Gaining that approval means that employees are more likely to be treated consistently in similar situations. While gaining those approvals, you may hear some advice on how to handle your problem employee which will be easier on you and fairer to the employee.

"Being conscious of the different Phases, makes it clearer what to do–Five-Phase Awareness.

"Sometimes, in a 'Dutch Uncle' Phase 3 discussion, you may become upset with an employee and be inclined to jump into Phase 4. Instead of taking that big leap, a cooling-down period for both of you gives the employee time to think it over and to be more responsive to your requests. In other words, it pays to keep your cool. This is true even if you're the owner of a company and don't need anyone else's approval.

"If after a cooling-off period, you're still not getting the response you need, you'll be able to plan better for approaching the employee in Phase 4.

"There will be documentation before and after the Phase 4 discussion. You'll give the employee a letter that covers what you're saying so that there will be no misunderstanding of how things stand. It is usually best to deliver that letter at the time of the conversation."

Ed looked at Angus Cassidy. "Does that answer your question?"

"Got it," said Angus.

Most of the class was nodding, but Maria Parker's face gave no expression as she made some notes.

"There's a tool available to you in Phase 4," said Ed. "It's called a PIP, a Personal Improvement Proposal. Before you give the employee your letter, you ask the employee to prepare a letter addressed to you that explains how they propose to improve. It's effective in getting the employee to focus on their own problem and what they are going to do about it. Their letter is often more powerful than your own. There is more about PIP in the notes I'll pass out. PIP isn't for everyone, but you will find it works well with most professional or administrative people.

Angus raised his hand. "Now that sounds like something that would work all the time."

"Sounds like it," said Ed, "but when we get to the case studies, you'll see that it doesn't always fit the circumstances. Okay, on to the next phase.

"**Phase 5**, 'Probation'. It's easy to tell when you're there, but it can be a lot of work. After being straightforward in Phase 3 and 4, if performance does not improve, entering Phase 5 will not be a surprise to the employee. That means that most of the stress will be avoided.

"Your conversation could go as smoothly as this: 'Sam, you've missed another report deadline. You know that forces us into probation. I've written out the conditions. Look at them. I'd appreciate your comments. The thing you're failing in is so clear, that the conditions of probation state that if you miss a weekly reporting deadline more than once in the next three months, you'll be fired. That would be a shame because you have a lot of other talents, but I realize you don't want another position. I wish you luck in this.'

"Probation is always done in writing with specific requirements for measurable results. The employee may argue that he has improved and try to outmaneuver you by making it uncomfortable for you to enter Phase 5. They may ask for an informal probation. They may want 'one last chance'. Probation *is* one last chance. After all, you haven't totally given up on this employee. You're willing to work with him–if he'll perform.

"If you made the mistake of placing the employee on an informal probation, and they failed, and now you have totally given up on the employee, then you have waited too long to put them on formal probation. The formal probationary period would become a charade–just going through the motions."

Ed looked around the room, "You've all seen cases like that."

Maria Parker, with her arms crossed once again, didn't even raise her hand to be recognized. "They're all like that," she said. "Every one I've ever seen or heard about."

"Not unlikely," said Ed. "And what does that mean? It means that the manager has been too slow in taking action. He's already made up his mind. Remember this: *Anytime you feel certain of the outcome of a phase you are about to enter, then you've waited too long to enter that phase.* You've wasted your own time, and you've wasted the time of your other employees who have to carry the workload until your PE starts to perform."

Maria pursed her lips and nodded.

Ed continued, "After Phase 5 the employee will either go back to work or be terminated. If they go back to work, they will be considered a normal employee, that is if the problems leading up to probation have been resolved. However, the employee may be marginal in performance or unstable in behavior and may have to be watched carefully. We'll discuss how to handle that situation later without enduring endless warnings or threats."

Maria squirmed in her chair. "What are the odds of an employee getting through each of the Phases?" she asked.

Ed turned to the class, "Anyone want to guess?"

Angus, a statistician by training, blurted out, "Ninety percent, ninety percent, eighty, ten, one."

Ed smiled. "Not bad. Probably as good a set of probabilities as anyone could construct.

"Actually, no statistics exist. But we know this: if a manager follows the guidelines, an employee in Phase 3 has an excellent chance of being successful. If a Phase 4 conversation is required, then the odds for success go down drastically because the employee has shown that he requires blunt conversation before he will respond. Like a mule, he needed a two-by-four to get his attention. However, if it's the first time the employee has entered Phase 4, and he successfully responds, then perhaps he will not become an habitual PE. Handling habitual PE's requires consideration, care, and excruciating clarity. More on such cases later.

"Phase 5 success is even rarer. By that time the employee has already had several chances. Angus's guess of one percent is probably a good one. There aren't any specific statistics because so much depends on how well the employee understood what was expected in the earlier stages. How well did the manager and the employee communicate? Human relationships always play a factor. If the employee has already been on 'informal' probation and you've already given up on them, then even one percent is probably too high.

"Now back to the question: 'What Phase was Walt Bramlett in?'"

Angus spoke first, "Not in one of your Phases. 'e was in a limbo phase. The icy isolation phase."

The class laughed and so did Ed. "If he wasn't in a Phase, then which Phases had he been through?" Ed asked.

"Maybe Phase 1 and 2," said Angus, "but he couldn't 'ave been in Phase 3 or 4 or 5 or 'e would 'ave known what the score was."

"No," said Maria, "He never had a help Phase or he would have understood the problem. Bramlett and his boss were such good friends, Julius probably couldn't even give Walt help in a straightforward manner."

"Good insight," said Ed. "The most unfair of all management actions and a very unusual one. Walt Bramlett was fired because his boss never helped him.

"What did Julius do? Remember?"

"He just hinted," said Maria.

"Right," said Ed, " He hinted. At least, he thought he gave hints. But the hints weren't good enough, and then Julius got frustrated and fired Walt for not accepting his hints. Was Walt so stupid he couldn't take a hint? No. I knew Walt and he wasn't stupid. It was simply that Julius was so concerned about upsetting his friend that he chose to be indirect, and he was so indirect, so unable to express himself like a Dutch Uncle, that he fired a friend."

"You said this really happened?" asked a voice from the back of the room. "A CEO of a big firm did that?"

"Yes," said Ed, "Like many fast-moving executives today, Julius was not trained in management. He was a natural at most aspects of business but a failure in some aspects of handling people. In this case, he made a fatal error. He did not 'discuss' the problem with Walt.

"Julius had almost done what so many managers do, go directly from over-doing the 'help' phases to Phase 6, firing. But Julius did worse than most managers. He skipped the 'help' phases. Not purposely, but he did.

"Let's see," said Ed, "how it looked to each of the parties involved.

"To Julius Redding: He loved having Walt, his old friend, working beside him. Walt knew aircraft like few did. He had an intuitive sense about their design and especially about selecting the right people who would be most successful in conceiving and developing advanced concepts. However, after Walt became Vice Chairman of the Board and became more involved with the management of the company, he had increased his attention to financial matters.

"Unlike many modern CEO's, Julius did not like getting into financial details and relied heavily on his Vice President of Finance. That made Julius uneasy when Walt came up with recommendations that were not readily accepted by the new V.P. of Finance. It caused conflict in an area that was uncomfortable to Julius. He preferred Walt to be out of such matters, especially when the V.P. of Finance became aggravated by Walt's 'interest'. Julius started by hinting to Walt that he should not get involved. Over time, he sniped at Walt's interference, always, however, trying to be friendly about it. Walt never understood the hints.

"It created stress and soon Julius found that it was easier to avoid Walt than to include him. The exclusion led to Walt being assigned to perfunctory tasks–ceremonial ones–until Walt could learn to comply. When after two years, it became a matter of embarrassment that Walt was kept out of most meetings, Julius finally spun the propellor and let Walt go. He did it in the most humane way he knew how. He assigned the matter to Ed Gannon." (Remember, throughout the story, Ed used fictitious names for himself and the other characters.)

"How it looked to Walt Bramlett: He thought Julius ignored financial matters more than he should, so Walt kept an eye open, trying to lower the risk of Julius receiving damaging surprises. Walt knew, without a doubt, that he was performing a beneficial and necessary service for Julius. Walt took Julius's jibes as indications that Julius was at least aware of his activities. Walt realized that at times Julius was uncomfortable about the debates that took place with the V.P. of Finance, who, being relatively new to the company, lacked some confidence, but Walt was certain that Julius must appreciate the net results–that things were getting a necessary airing. After all, Walt was protecting Julius. If Julius were to fail in his responsibilities, Walt would be his most likely successor. Walt never understood why he was increasingly excluded from key meetings. Then he felt the tension and the complete withdrawal of Julius. He had asked Julius what was wrong but Julius always avoided giving a straight answer. After two years of isolation, Walt was fired."

The class members looked around at each other.

Ed continued, "And this is how it appeared to the rest of the Executive Staff: They liked Walt but they were relieved when Julius finally fired him. They didn't like the tension that existed when Julius and Walt were together or when Julius was trying to avoid Walt. In spite of their respect for Walt, they were glad to have the matter finally resolved.

"The V.P. of Finance looked at it differently. He lacked confidence, so he didn't like Walt looking over his shoulder. In order to avoid Walt's scrutiny, Mr. Finance exaggerated Walt's interference. Later, Mr. Finance failed to recognize that Walt's exclusion in all matters was a result of his own complaints.

"Ed Gannon: We've already witnessed his assessment. Julius Redding was a friendly man but not one you could trust with your career.

"The truth was that Julius Redding was a fine man. In most things. He was easy-going, courageous, and loyal to his friends. His career had progressed in a rough environment where managers did not readily discuss personnel actions. They just did what was 'necessary' and charged ahead. They were pioneers in their field, and raised another generation of executives who saw personnel matters the same way–something to be handled or mishandled expeditiously. There were few laws to impede them.

"But what Julius did to Walt was not expeditious. It was excruciatingly ineffective, and two years in hell for everyone. Julius had never heard of Phase 3 so he never had that straightforward talk with Walt. Julius just kept 'helping' in the only way he knew–by friendly sniping–and then, when baffled and irritated, Julius became silent and aloof. He assumed that Walt understood.

"Julius lost two years and a trusted advisor and friend. Walt lost his dignity, the fun of contributing, and then his job."

A voice in the back of the class asked, "I'd like to hear what Julius should have said to Walt."

"Anyone?" asked Ed.

"Simple. This would be Phase 1," said Angus, "Hey, Walt, yuh got me feelin' uneasy, mon. These issues you keep raisin' with finance 'ave got to stop. I trust Mr. Finance and he's gettin' mighty upset. I'd be bloody happy if you'd keep your hands off. Would yuh do that now?"

Ed laughed. "Exactly. It allows Walt to explain himself–that he was acting in Julius's best interest. Then, if Julius insisted, Walt might have complied, in fact happily, because finance was not one of Walt's loves. On the other hand, Walt might have considered what he was doing as imperative to his position on the Board. They might have had a good debate and it might have resulted in Julius agreeing with Walt, or in Walt resigning. Either way, the issue would have been resolved without two years of growing animosity.

"So it went from 'hint, hint' to withdrawal and then, 'We want you to retire'.

"Go into Phase 3 when you first recognize the unusual. It will save you time and energy. It will lead to more happy endings. If the ending is not one of successful employment, it will at least reach termination faster. And that's also good for everyone."

Angus raised his hand. "Ed," he said, "you seem to know a lot of the details of what 'appened."

"Yes, I came to know all three of the people involved." I was one of them, Ed said to himself, and then continued talking before Angus could ask the next obvious question, 'How did you know all of this?'

Several other hands were raised, but Ed waved them off. "We're going to stop for the day," he said. "Here are a few pages of notes that summarize what we've talked about. They'll answer some of the questions that haven't been asked.

"Next week, when we meet for our final session, we'll discuss nine cases that will illustrate how to use the Five Phase approach."

"The Cat of Nine Tales," said a voice from the back.

Ed smiled, then nodded. "The cases are short. Nine of them in ninety minutes, so arrive alert. Then, we'll answer any questions. Have a good week. See you next Saturday."

A few minutes earlier, in the back of the room, the Vice President of Human Resources had quietly entered to deliver some disturbing news to Ed. As the class filed out, he slowly approached.

Chapter 4

Guilty

Ed spoke first. "Hal, you look like a sad-eyed bloodhound."

"Not good news," said Hal, "Bob Parker called me last night and came to my home this morning. It's about you."

"His niece was in class today," said Ed, "First time I've met her. Maria's quite a skeptic."

"Not generally," said Hal, "but she can be blunt. She's smart. Anyway, it's nothing she would have said."

"So?"

"Parker grilled me on one subject. He asked what I thought of the hours you spent in class, how much time it took to prepare, how much value was it, and whether someone else couldn't do it."

Ed stood ramrod straight, looking into Hal's eyes.

"I gave him every positive answer I could," said Hal. "I told him how important it was that a man in your position would take the time to impress on your managers a new approach to management effectiveness. I told him that you wouldn't have to do this forever, but you were needed for the first year or two.

"He challenged me on that. He said that high level executives don't normally teach in Management Development classes. I explained that this was different because we were the first company I knew of to promote the Five Phase approach. If we weren't the first, then your attendance wouldn't be necessary."

"Right," said Ed.

"But Parker said maybe you shouldn't be taking the time to pioneer it. We argued a while on that. He even seemed to buy the logic." Hal hesitated, looking at Ed.

"I know," said Ed, "the point is he thinks it's important enough to investigate. So, it's of real concern, maybe to him, maybe to others on the committee."

"He didn't state his position. I'm not sure he's the one giving it so much weight. He did say, though, that he realized I was bound to be positive about your participation."

Ed nodded. "So, essentially, he was willing to discount everything you said unless you came up with something negative. He would have accepted that. You didn't give him an easy out. He still has to weigh it." Ed smiled. "One thing for sure: my class time is an issue."

"I don't know how you can counter it," said Hal. "Supposedly you don't even know this has come up."

Chapter 5

The Notes

Late that evening, Maria Parker took off her hat and sat down in an easy chair with Ed's notes. She felt disappointed in herself for revealing her skepticism in class. She knew she had been excessively influenced by her uncle's request for her opinion of the Five Phase approach and why it required an Executive Vice President to teach it.

If Ed had known that one of the evaluators would be reading his notes when he was being considered as a candidate for president, he might not have written them in such a casual manner.

Maria began reading.

* * * * * * * * * * * * *

Five Phase Quick Reference

These notes are a brief introduction to the Five Phases. They cover the following subjects:

1) The Correct Time to Enter Each Phase.
2) Signs That You Have Waited Too Long to Enter a Phase.
3) How Long To Spend in Each Phase.
4) Documentation For Each Phase.
5) Discussion With Your Management.
6) Following Company Policy. Union Contracts.

*　　　*　　　*　　　*　　　*

1) The Correct Time to Enter Each Phase.

Phase 1 and 2. You don't know you're in Phase 1 or 2. You are offering normal help.

Phase 3. You wonder what's wrong because your employee is not responding satisfactorily to your help. If you can't think of a reason, you are ready to enter Phase 3.

Do so by expressing your concern in a manner that will be most conducive to a positive turnaround by the employee. *Above all, DO NOT HESITATE TO ENTER PHASE 3. DELAY IS THE MOST COMMON MISTAKE.*

You will be giving the employee the benefit of every doubt; you will be asking what can be done to improve performance. If the employee gives reasonable responses and you are encouraged that performance will improve, you will continue in Phase 3 by offering whatever help you feel is necessary.

Phase 4. If the employee does not give reasonable responses to your Phase 3 discussion, and you encounter a stream of excuses, or a bad attitude, or other unsatisfactory reaction, then you are probably seriously concerned about the employee's performance and you should prepare to enter Phase 4. (You might also arrive at Phase 4 after a positive Phase 3 discussion, but followed by continued lack of satisfactory improvement.)

PREPARATION FOR PHASE 4. It is time to have a serious discussion with the employee. First, do two things:

(1) Briefly document the history of help given to the employee and the employee's response to the Phase 3 session. If there are previous performance appraisals, review them. Write a letter to the employee–which you will hand deliver when you meet with them–that describes the nature of the problem and what the employee must do to correct it.

(2) Review the documentation with your immediate manager. (Even if you owned the company, the documentation would be helpful to your thinking and preparation.) Let your manager know of your plans for the Phase 4 discussion. If you have a Human Resources Department–and we do–discuss the situation with them in keeping with company policy. At this point, you may decide that when you meet with the employee you will ask the employee to prepare a PIP, a Personal Improvement Proposal. It is the employee's effort to

describe what they will do to improve so that they can avoid being placed on probation.

Remember, two heads are better than one in such matters. Another perspective, including that of the employee, may reveal a better way of working with the employee and therefore a better chance for the employee to succeed.

Then, and only then, are you prepared to see the employee and "Show Serious Concern. Discuss it." In fairness to the employee, the discussion and the letter must express the seriousness of the situation in non-ambiguous terms. It cannot be like Julius Redding's hints. That's why we say, not only "show" serious concern, but also "discuss" the concern. The employee must know that if performance does not improve, probation or dismissal will follow.

After your discussion, if PIP is the path you have chosen, you might decide to give the employee your letter or you might decide to first let them write their PIP. In either case, you will give them time to prepare their proposal before you meet again. Sometimes their plan is so well written, including a clear statement of the problem as well as how the deficiency will be corrected, that it is unnecessary to deliver the letter which you had previously prepared.

Depending on the circumstances, you may continue to offer help during Phase 4. However, the emphasis must be on the employee taking responsibility for improvement, which means that the employee may receive less help or no help at all. To be fairly measured, they should generally receive no more help than others, and no less.

Phase 5. The employee who has not responded adequately in Phase 4 is placed on formal probation. This is done by following company procedures. If none were to exist, a written letter would still have to be given to the employee, and discussed with the employee, to ensure complete understanding of what must be accomplished. At this point, a previously written PIP might be of help. Milestones must be included to ensure that progress is being made toward the ultimate completion. Some of those milestones may be designated *in advance* as intermediate decision points. Those are points at which, if the employee is not on schedule, a decision will be made to fire the employee without completing the entire probationary period. It is equal to failure on the project because missing that milestone would make it impossible to meet the final schedule or results.

*　　　　　*　　　　　*

2) *Signs That You've Waited Too Long to Enter a Phase.*

Phase 1 or 2. Examples: 1) The production line collapsed due to inadequate training of the employee or due to inadequate performance, 2) Laboratory tests were invalidated again because procedures were not followed, and critical schedules will now be missed, 3) Faulty programming documentation resulted in the team missing another important milestone.

Phase 3. You have given the employee so much help that you have become totally frustrated with the employee, or fellow employees are irritated to the extent that they just want the employee to disappear. They've given up on him. In other words, you are past the point where you can have a legitimate "Dutch Uncle" talk–you would be *pretending* that you have an open mind.

Phase 4. You have mistakenly given the employee *every conceivable* chance to prove himself in Phase 3 and now you have no hope that he can do the job. You have subjected yourself, the employee, and the employee's fellow workers to an unnecessarily grueling experience. Now you are boxed in and must repeat what you have been through by formally entering Phase 4 and then Phase 5. Unfortunately, you are already convinced of the negative outcome.

Phase 5. Similar to Phase 4. You are sure the employee will fail because you've already put the employee through all the hoops but without putting him on formal probation. Now, you must repeat the process and formally document it so that the employee has a supposedly "fair" chance to respond, and your company is protected from a lawsuit.

(Note: Situations like this–where you stay too long in Phase 3 or 4–lead employees to feel that they are not being given a fair chance once they finally do go on probation. Actually, you probably gave them that chance earlier, perhaps at their own request when they asked for 'one more chance' before probation. But your attitude now causes them to be angry with you and the company. They sense correctly that your mind is already made up. They may want to go to court. You had good intentions, but as the philosopher said, "The road to hell is paved with good intentions." You *are* now the bad guy. Everyone has to suffer again while you go through a perfunctory documented probationary period.)

*   *   *

3) How Long to Spend in Each Phase.
There is no fixed amount of time.

It can range from a few seconds per phase to several months. Some things are simplistic and some complex. Your judgment is required. The employee who is habitually disturbing others while they are working is easier to judge than is the contribution of a single programmer, in a team of programmers, in the design of a new programming language. The disturbances can be easily observed and judged, but the programmer's work may take months to fairly evaluate.

*   *   *

4) Documentation For Each Phase.
Phase 1 and 2. No documentation.

Phase 3. Usually, no documentation is necessary. However, if the Phase 3 discussion results in the manager having misgivings, then the manager will want to document the help given in Phase 1 and 2 as well as the Phase 3 conversation. If later, it becomes necessary to enter Phase 4, this documentation will become useful in aiding your memory and in fulfilling the need to "Document the earlier history."

Phase 4.

A) Document the earlier history.

B) Prepare a letter which you will give to the employee, stating in clear terms what must be corrected or accomplished.

C) Discuss A and B above with your manager and Human Resources.

D) Meet with the employee and conduct the "serious" discussion.

E) If you have decided to ask the employee to write a PIP, that should be requested of them now.

F) Meet again with the employee for the second part of your discussion. Read the PIP and discuss it. It may be adequate, but if not you may ask the employee to try another rewrite with the help of your suggestions. Once the PIP is satisfactory, you can agree on it and then, if it is still necessary, give the employee a copy of the letter which you have previously written. The employee should sign a copy. (If the employee is unable or unwilling to prepare a satisfactory PIP, do not force the issue further, just document what you have.)

G) Document the meetings you have just held, including what action has been decided.

Phase 5. Full documentation including:

a) all previous documentation.

b) detailed description of work to be done in the probationary period and how it will be evaluated to determine success or failure. The PIP letter may serve as a good reference.

The package must be reviewed in advance by your boss and the Human Resources department and must clearly spell out the consequences of failure. That may be dismissal from the company, demotion, transfer, or…?

*   *   *

5) Discussion With Your Own Management.
Phase 1, 2, 3. No discussion necessary.
Phase 4, 5. Seek advice and consent as mentioned in the paragraphs above.

6) Following Company Policy. Union Contracts.
If you adhere to the spirit of the Five Phases, you will be on solid ground. When you first talk to your boss or to the Human Resources Department about a problem employee, you can expect their first question to be, "What Phase are you in?" If you can't answer that question, they will wonder where you have been.

We don't have any unions, but if we ever did we would attempt to convince the union to allow us to use this straightforward approach. If we couldn't convince them, we might have to modify our philosophy beginning with Phase 4. That would be unfortunate.

*   *   *   *   *   *   *

I hope that Five-Phase Awareness will help you better enjoy your management experience.

Your fellow manager,

Ed Gannon

* * * * * * * * * * * * * * *

Maria leaned back in her chair and momentarily closed her eyes. She placed the notes in her briefcase and wondered if the process really worked as cleanly as advertised. What about extreme cases? How would those be handled? Was that part of what he would answer with his nine case studies? Ed, in his basketball days, had become known as "The Cat," because of the way he pounced on a loose ball. That had led to classes calling him "The Cat of Nine Tales." Now, she would be listening to all nine of them.

Chapter 6

Not Changing Horses

The following Saturday, just before Ed entered the classroom, he received a phone call from Hal.

"Ed, the issue is still alive. The other two members of the Search Committee called me. They asked the same questions. I thought you might want to reconsider. You could finish the session today, then announce that it was your last class."

"I'm not getting off my horse in mid stream," said Ed.

Hal hesitated. "No surprise. One last input. You may not be able to sway Maria Parker, but she and Angus Cassidy are professional friends. She values his judgment."

"Thanks," said Ed. "I don't think that changes a thing I might say, but I'll keep it in mind." He still couldn't read Maria. Good poker player. Ed picked up his notes and walked into the classroom.

He saw Maria and Angus talking. In every class, a handful of people led the questioning. In this one, it was Maria and Angus.

He put his notes on the lectern. "Good morning," he said, "A nice Saturday morning to you all. Were the 'Quick Reference' notes helpful?"

A bearded first-line supervisor raised his hand. "I'm known as a pretty easy-going guy. How do I tell if I'm giving too much help?"

"Who has an answer?" asked Ed.

Angus spoke up, "When you jolly well feel like it."

"And what if my troops think I'm helping too much?" asked the supervisor.

Angus again answered. "You better not let 'em get too restless, or you'll lose 'em all. But if you think you're doing the right thing, and you're not just being a good natured wimp, then stick to your belief, my man, and 'elp, 'elp, 'elp. Just make sure you don't 'elp yourself to death."

There was laughter throughout the classroom, but the supervisor looked around and saw that Angus's comments were accepted.

Maria added, "If you keep communications open with your people, they'll let you know."

"Other questions?" asked Ed.

"Yes," replied Maria, and then asked what several participants had on their mind. "Outside the classroom, you insist on brevity. And it seems like you're focusing on what happens after a manager gives help. Why do you have two help phases? Or even one? Why didn't you call it 4 phases or 3?"

"Good," said Ed, "Even though we're concentrating in this class on phases 3 through 5, I don't want anyone to forget about help. That's why it's in there twice.

"If the employee can be helped, it's best all around. It's another example of 'Good personnel policy is good for everyone, including the manager'. The libraries are full of books telling managers how to help. There are volumes explaining the details of probation. However, there's nothing on the concept of Five Phases and nothing on how all Five Phases are tied together, or when to proceed from one phase to another. Thanks for asking."

"I was just a shill?" asked Maria, good naturedly.

"Other questions?" asked Ed with a smile.

A bald-headed man sitting in the front row raised his hand and made his comment in a careful manner. "I was surprised that under probation you mention transfer as a possible consequence of failing. I've always thought of that as the coward's way out–just passing a problem to someone else."

"If you have a person in the wrong job, you have a responsibility to move that person," said Ed. "That might mean a demotion or firing or transfer. Something.

"If the employee is talented with the right attitude, a transfer might be exactly the right thing. It will save a good person for the company. The transfer might also carry a demotion with it. Some managers, just as you implied, never recommend a transfer because they're afraid they'll be considered a coward. That makes them cowards."

Ed looked at the man who had made the comment. "And I'm not accusing you of being a coward. You probably saw some transfers being made where a manager wrapped up his PE in a nice package and gave him to some unsuspecting soul, and you came to view all transfers as the wrong thing to do. It's not unsound if you're transferring for the right reasons and if everyone involved—most often including the receiving manager—is aware of the situation.

"Whether you choose firing or demotion, or any other consequence, you have to question your own reasoning. And unless you're alone in the world, your manager and Human Resources also have to question you. It's an important decision to the employee and the company. You might be talking about a five-year professional with considerable knowledge. It would be costly to replace that training. It's up to you to see how to salvage that person and their talent.

"It's true that when you consider transfer you have to look into yourself much more deeply. However, once you've seen how easy it is to use the Five Phases, you won't be fearful in confronting a problem employee. Once that fear is gone, you won't have to second guess yourself so much when you think that a transfer is the right option.

"In the cases we're going to look at, remember to ask yourself about the problem employees, if you would fire them, demote them, or transfer them. We'll discuss it.

"Let's go to the Cases."

Case 1

Too Long to Eat

Ed passed out the case study.

*   *   *   *   *   *   *

Case 1

Background: Monday, a new employee joined your group. Tuesday, he took three hours for lunch. You immediately advised him that in your department people operated as a team and must be present when the other team members were there; lunches were limited to one hour. You did not express 'concern'. Wednesday, the employee returned from lunch in one hour.

Today, Thursday: The employee again took three hours for lunch.

What Phase are you in? What are you going to do?

        *   *   *   *   *   *   *

When they were finished reading, Ed asked, "Who has an answer?"

A red headed supervisor raised his hand, a smile on his face, and Ed nodded to him. "It's time to put him on probation," he said.

The bearded supervisor who had described himself as easy-going, spoke up. "No," he said, "you've only helped him once. You need to explain it to him again. He'll be in Phase 2."

The red head raised his hand. "Maybe this is a place for a PIP letter. Let the guy write up his own problem."

"Maybe," said Angus, "but this is a joke. It was a simple thing you asked. 'e's testing you. You shouldn't push him too slow or too fast. 'e may have some talent you need. Not knowing about his skill level, I'd 'ave a Phase 3 discussion with 'im, and somewhere in the middle of that polite give and take, I'd shift right into Phase 4. I'd let the mon know that we didn't cater to such mischief. He's 'ad enough 'elp with the first conversation. 'e don't need no more 'elp. 'e needs a 'it in the 'ead. Probation is too fast. More 'elp is too slow."

"I agree with that," said Maria, "except I'd avoid the Phase 4 part of the discussion unless I saw that his attitude was bad. Then I'd do it, even though I know you said to talk over Phase 4 with your manager before you do it."

"Right," said Ed, "I said there were exceptions. And this might be one of them. Not taking three hour lunches is simple to understand. We've talked about being aware of what Phase you're in. We also said not to spend an unnecessary amount of time in any Phase.

"You've got it right. More help is unnecessary. Phase 3 is mandatory to clear the air. You make sure that the importance of what you said is understood. Easing into Phase 4 is a real possibility, but it will depend on the employee's attitude. One more time, and you'll probably be into Phase 4 and 5 at the same time. The idea of jumping directly to a PIP letter has a lot of merit. Either way you do it, it probably won't allow for more than three occurrences, of something so simple, before the employee is on probation."

Case 2

Repeat Offense

Background: A week later, you placed the three-hour-lunch employee on probation for 90 days. Probation was successfully passed yesterday.

Today: The employee took a three hour lunch.

What Phase are you in? What do you do?

*   *   *   *   *   *   *

When everyone had finished reading the case, Ed looked quizzically at the class.

"Fire him," said the redhead.

The easy-going bearded manager realized he had been too easy before. "Go directly to Phase 3," he said.

"Put 'im back on 90-day probation," said Angus.

The class looked at each other, somewhat uncomfortable with any of the answers. They looked to Ed.

"You could probably fire him and win in court. But we're not looking for legal disputes.

"He has already shown by his successful time on probation that he doesn't need to have anything explained to him.

"If he's a marginal employee, you might just tell him that he is on perpetual probation and will receive a letter shortly. In that letter, you might add that–because of his marginal performance–if he should break any other company policies that are perceived as testing management's authority, that he will be on perpetual probation for all such issues and may be fired without further warning.

"If he's a valuable worker, you might want to compliment him on having outsmarted you. Then tell him he's on perpetual probation and not to try testing you on anything else."

"Good," said Angus, "you don't 'ave to start all over."

"No need to waste your time," said Ed. He noticed that even Maria's hat was bobbing up and down.

"We talked about situations where it might be right to transfer an employee. Transfer this one?" asked Ed.

"Of course not," said the easy-going bearded supervisor, to show that he was learning.

"That was a trap question," said Ed. "You always have to look beyond the obvious. That's why these situations require your personal judgment, case by case. There are no pat answers. What if this was an outstanding employee and you learned, or guessed, that his behavior was a reaction to you personally? If you couldn't get along, transferring might be the right thing to do.

"That's a hard one for most managers to accept–that some employees don't work well for them, but might work well for others. If their work history is good, you might place some blame on yourself–at least question yourself. However, if you transfer them, knowing that their work history is poor, you are contributing to an ongoing problem.

"Most attitude cases, you won't decide to transfer. Somebody might want Dennis Rodman, but it's not up to you to find them. Let Dennis go out and find his own team. Let them take the risk as to whether or not they'll still have a team after he arrives. Maybe they will and maybe they won't."

Case 3

A Career on Probation

Background: Your name is Gladys and you have taken over a new department. Two levels of management report to you and a total of 50 professionals. After three hectic months of digesting your responsibilities, you notice that one of the staff engineers has been on probation for seven months. The second-level manager tells you that the first-level manager has everything under control but that they have to be careful with the "PE" because in the past he has written letters to the corporate president–appealing probationary or disciplinary actions on three different occasions and winning each appeal. This time, they want to "nail him." He is an inadequate performer who has been transferred all over the organization.

Two months go by and the man is still on probation. You look deeper into the case. He has been on and off probation for 14 years. The first time was three months after he joined the company. Shortly after being placed on probation that first time, he was transferred to the company's primary maintenance site. He has since been promoted three times, but not in the last ten years.

You talk to some of his most recent managers–managers whom you know by reputation to be good technical leaders. Each one of them revealed the same story: They met the PE while he was working for his previous manager, and the PE asked to be transferred to them. They accepted. Sometimes the PE even got a promotion for the move. In a few months the new manager discovered that the PE had major skill shortcomings and continually offered excuses for his lack of productivity. When the new manager made it clear he would no longer accept excuses, the PE would explain, "You are not capable of evaluating my work. There is another manager who has that capability and I would like you to transfer me to him." They invariably did.

Today: The PE's second-level manager tells you that they need to lengthen the probationary period by another 30 days because the PE has another excuse. The manager is afraid that if they do not extend probation that the employee would win on appeal.

What do you do?

*   *   *   *   *   *   *

"Call the SOB in and watch while the manager tells 'im what has to be done during probation. Make sure it's clear. No ambiguity," said Angus. "You can't let this go on."

"Get the Human Resources Manager to help make sure the probationary requirements are spelled out properly," said the bearded supervisor.

The redheaded supervisor shook his head. "It's time to fire him," he said. "It's gone on too long. If you have to, you get Human Resources and even the president, to agree in advance. Then do it. Fire him."

Maria's head was shaking. "No," she said, "You can't expect the president to get involved in every case in advance. The immediate management has to be able to handle it." The class nodded agreement. "Certainly not in a company our size," she added.

"Is this from a real case?" asked Angus.

"Yes," replied Ed. "They all are."

"What 'appened?" asked Angus.

"Gladys met with the two levels of management over the PE. She found the probationary requirements were difficult to spell out. She asked that the tasks be broken down into smaller segments that could be more precisely measured. She insisted that the PE, before continuing on probation would have to agree with the performance requirements of each step, and would also have to agree that if a step was missed that the entire project schedule or quality would be missed.

"Gladys then asked her subordinate managers if the PE understood the consequences of failure–that he would be fired. The managers said 'Yes'. Then she asked if they had ever used the word "fire" with the PE. They looked at each other, then sheepishly responded, 'No'.

"They all agreed that Gladys should meet with the employee, with the other two managers present, along with a Human Resources representative, and Gladys would use the word 'fire'.

"They met in a conference room. The PE was as calm as though resting on a riverbank, waiting for a fish to bite. Nothing Gladys said to him disturbed his tranquility. The PE agreed that all the intermediate tasks were reasonable and that missing any one of them would constitute missing the final required result. The PE was near comatose, sighing a few times as though bored.

"Then, Gladys asked him, 'Do you know the consequences of failure?' The PE casually nodded his head. He had been through this so many times before.

"The first-level and second-level managers appeared nervous, wondering if Gladys had forgotten to say 'fire'.

"Then, Gladys asked him, 'Do you know that if you fail, you will be fired?'

"The PE squirmed to an upright position in his chair. He looked at Gladys. His eyes began to water. It was the first time he appeared to recognize that something important was happening that could affect his future. He nodded that he understood.

"Three weeks before a critical checkpoint, the PE called Gladys to announce that he was resigning. He had found a position with more pay at another company.

"Six months later, the PE called Gladys to say how happy he was at his new company and that he wished he had left Gladys's company a long time ago. The new company was a competitor.

"The balding manager who had first questioned transferring an employee, spoke up, "That's the kind of situation that gives transferring a bad name."

"No doubt," said Ed. "There's a right time to transfer and a wrong time. The managers who transferred this PE for 14 years were all technically good. They were also busy. They took the quick way out. When the employee feathered his next nest in advance, it was too easy for them to agree to the transfer. Their real responsibility, for the good of the company, was to release the PE if he could not perform.

"Each case is unique. Each requires judgment. A PIP letter might have been good earlier in the man's career, but by the time Gladys came on the scene it was far too late. Remember, we don't have any pat answers, just a process that works. Next case."

Case 4

The Shootout

Background: None.

Today: An employee brought a concealed gun to work, got into an argument, and took the gun out of his desk. It accidentally discharged. A light fixture was damaged.

What Phase are you in? What do you do?

*   *   *   *   *   *   *

"Phase 6," shouted Angus. "The mon's in jail. 'e has been fired."

"Any other suggestions?" asked Ed.

The class was still.

"Again," said Ed, "You need to know what Phase you're in, but extreme conditions can cause you to go through a number of Phases very quickly. The PE went through every Phase in the instant he pulled that weapon out, in the instant it was brandished in anger. Next case."

Case 5

On a Slow Train

Background: The Information Technology (IT) Manager has come to the Human Resources (HR) Manager for agreement to fire a programmer. The IT Manager displayed a letter that was given to the programmer five months ago placing her on 90-day probation.

The letter appears to clearly define what is expected of the programmer–at least as clearly as one can reasonably describe such work. It tells the PE, "You are guaranteed the cooperation of your fellow workers." Later, the letter states, "Action, not excuses, is expected of you."

The following conversation took place today:

HR Manager: "I should ask you why you didn't see me before writing that letter. But, why are you here after 150 days instead of the 90 in the letter?"

IT Manager: "The programmer thinks that, under the circumstances, she did as well as could be expected. She felt she had met the test, so I gave her an additional 60 days."

HR: "In writing?"

IT: "No. Mistake, right?"

HR: "Right. Did she need the cooperation of the other programmers, and did she get it?"

IT: "She needed it but they were already too fed up with her. That's why I've got to get her out. They want to get the work done themselves without her around. She's a nuisance."

*   *   *

What Phase was she in when she received the letter?

What Phase is she in now?

If you were the HR Manager what would you do?

* * * * * * *

Ed saw only one hand raised, the balding manager.

"She received a probationary letter, so she was in Phase 5," said Baldy. "She's still in Phase 5 until she's been fired. I'd approve of firing her, although I'd expect some kind of fight from her–maybe a discrimination suit."

No other hands were raised as the class looked around the room, obviously feeling uneasy.

Finally, Angus spoke up. "Right now she's in Phase 5 and a 'alf. She's been fired but she's still on the payroll. She knows that. The IT Manager knows it too."

The class laughed. But some nodded.

Ed asked Angus, "And where was she when the letter was written?"

Angus threw up his hands. "Probably on a three hour lunch," he said.

Ed smiled. "I meant what Phase was she in."

"I know," said Angus, "I suppose, way back then, she was already in Phase 5 and a 'alf."

"Why do you say that?" asked Ed.

Angus shrugged, but Maria spoke up. "It was the letter," she said, "it showed that the manager had already given up on her–that sentence, 'Action, not excuses, is expected of you'. She was as good as fired."

Ed nodded. "So what's your recommendation?" he asked.

"You can't fire her," said the redhead, "She was promised cooperation and didn't get it. The IT Manager promised it to her and admitted himself that she needed the cooperation to perform."

"You have to fire her," said the bearded supervisor, "Even a softie like me can see that. She's causing too much trouble with the other employees. They'll all resign if you don't get rid of her. You need to fire her and take your chances with a lawsuit."

The class argued the various views until Angus asked Ed, "What 'appened in the real case?"

"The HR Manager was also concerned about the letter," said Ed, "No one but the IT Manager had ever reviewed the letter before it was given to the employee. That was in violation of company policy, and in violation of good sense and good practice.

"The HR Manager pointed out that in the time period before the letter was written the employee had already exhausted the patience of the IT Manager and his people. The PE had never received a Phase 3 or Phase 4 discussion—she had been 'helped' by everyone until she was placed on a 'verbal probation'. It was uncertain how clearly the terms of the 'verbal probation' were spelled out. The lack of documentation ensured that there would be disagreement. When interviewed by an HR representative, the woman claimed that not everyone had been helpful to her, and in fact the letter supported her claim or it would not have been likely for the IT Manager to 'guarantee cooperation'.

"The HR Manager also pointed out that the IT Manager had made a promise that he couldn't keep—guaranteeing his employees' cooperation–and that he had acknowledged the need for cooperation which she didn't get, therefore the probationary period was doomed to failure. It was a waste of everyone's time because the employee, after 5 months, could prove that she was not given a fair chance, at least not during the probationary period.

"My soapbox now: *There is nothing so unfair to an employee as to not let them know where they stand.*

"In this case, it was evident that the employee, for a long time, did not know where she stood. She received considerable help from those around her until some of them became tired of it. They may have switched to actually making things difficult for her. She probably still didn't know the seriousness of her situation when she went into verbal probation. By the time she received the letter, everyone–including herself–was worn out and she felt that the written probation was unfair. It was. By trying to be overly nice, the manager had been unfair to everyone.

"Are you saying she got off?" asked the redhead.

"The IT Manager had exposed his team to this problem for over a year after most of them felt the PE was hopeless. If the woman was now fired, she would probably claim discrimination and continue to think that she was a qualified programmer. The HR Manager recommended that she be given a probationary assignment that she could do on her own, without anyone else's cooperation. Before delivering the new letter, HR management insisted on reviewing it. If she failed to meet the milestones, she would then be released."

"I can't believe it," said the bearded softie.

Ed looked at the bearded supervisor. "After digesting this class, be careful not to swing too far from your natural tendencies. If you were too tough before, don't make the mistake of always being too soft. And if you were too soft, don't automatically become tough. The message is to be fair. Express yourself to the employee as soon as you are aware that you should be in the next Phase. Keep your employees informed so that they don't have to fear that someday you might suddenly lose your patience and put them on probation–like this letter–or fire them."

The class sat silently, most of them nodding.

"What 'appened?" asked Angus.

"It was considered too late for a PIP letter. She was given a draft of her new probationary terms. She negotiated some minor changes. One month later, as the first major milestone approached, she resigned. At that time, she agreed that she was in the wrong profession.

"That's a much happier ending than if the company had fired her and she had wasted months or years fighting the case, only to find out later that she was not suited for programming.

"Any questions?

"On to the next case."

Case 6

Hangups

Background: You are Gilbert Smith, the Chief Product Manager for your company's products. The company attributes much of its success to high ethical standards and good customer relations. Periodically, you conduct sessions with all of your Product Managers in which you discuss management philosophy and principles.

Last month, you gave each participant a book in which you inscribed a note saying, "I hope this book will help guide your decision making."

Your product manager for "Model Z's," Spike Bizarre, read the book several times. For the last year, Spike has been facing extreme competitive pressure from a new product, called "Super Model," which is superior to Model Z for most applications. So far, the salespeople who work for Spike have managed to win most of their competitive battles but a momentous order is now in jeopardy at Spike's oldest and largest customer, "Bread and Butter, Incorporated." Spike has been trying to help the salesman on the account.

Today: Spike comes to Gilbert.

Spike: "I've reread that book you gave me."

Gil: "You look bothered by it."

Spike: "Bread and Butter wants my advice–whether to buy our Model Z or to buy Super Model. I don't know what to tell them."

Gil: (Trying to disguise his surprise.) "What have you told them so far?"

Spike: "I've just explained the advantages of Model Z."

Gil: "Good."

Spike: "But Super Model is really better."

Gil: "Isn't that for them to decide?"

Spike: "Sure, but they asked my opinion. I've always tried to present myself to them as a professional–more like an objective consultant than a sales manager. And now, if I follow the ethics of that book, it supports what I've always tried to do. Be honest."

Gil: "Until last year the Model Z was always superior, so it wasn't hard to be honest. Show me where the book says to make a decision for your customer."

Spike: "I don't think it does, but it says to be honest."

Gil: "Bread and Butter knows their requirement better than we do."

Spike: "True."

Gil: "Your responsibility is to present your product as honestly as you can, pointing out all of its advantages. It's up to them to make their own decision. (Gil then recounted for Spike all of the Model Z's advantages to make certain that none were being overlooked.) There are lots of reasons to pick the Model Z. Let the customer decide."

Spike: "I'm uncomfortable with that."

Gil: "Does the Account Rep on Bread and Butter feel you're giving him your full support?"

Spike: "I think so."

Tomorrow afternoon, Spike has a meeting scheduled with the customer to respond to their request for an opinion.

What Phase are you in? What do you do next?

* * * * * * *

Ed looked at the class and raised his eyebrows.

"You have to go through Phase 3, 4, and 5 right now," said the redhead. "He has to agree that he's going to do his best to sell his product, or he has to go. You can't let him see the customer in his present frame of mind."

"You can't take a chance," said the bearded softie, "You have to take him out of his job before he sees the customer."

"And what if the customer calls him after he doesn't show up?" asked Maria of the bearded one. "He's going to give the customer his opinion and tell them that his company wouldn't let him be honest. Then you've jeopardized the account."

Ed nodded.

"Gil has to try 'arder to convince Spike," said Angus.

"Assume Gil does that," said Ed. "He tries but fails."

The class argued the options until Angus again turned to Ed. "What really 'appened?" he asked.

"Gil asked Spike if he could make a living by making decisions for his customers.

"Spike, on reflection, said, 'Maybe not'.

"Gil responded, 'And your sales staff probably couldn't either'.

"Gil told Spike to go home and consider whether or not he belonged in sales. He told Spike that if he decided the answer was no, then Spike should try to transfer to another position within the company–with Gil's support if Gil thought it was a good fit–or to go outside the company.

"Gil asked Spike to come see him the first thing in the morning with his answer.

"In the morning, with bloodshot eyes, Spike requested a transfer. They agreed that Spike should go on sick leave until they could work out the change. That afternoon, Gil made the call on the customer.

"Spike was transferred to a creative position in marketing where his skills could be used and where he would not have to interface with customers."

"Whew!" said Angus.

"So all the Phases were bypassed," said the softie bearded manager.

"Not really," said Ed. "In the one conversation, Gilbert Smith moved from helping Spike with his thinking, to giving Spike alternatives that were certainly Phase 4 in nature. Serious. There was no time to consult with the next level of management. Gil was very conscious of where he was in the phases. The situation called for a quick resolution without risking company objectives, and it was still fair to Spike. Agree?"

A majority of the class nodded their heads.

"It shows again," said Ed, "as I stand here on my soap box, that what is fair to an employee can almost always be made fair to the company. Where conflict appears it is the responsibility of management to find a convergence of objectives. In this case, Gil was able to help Spike escape from an uncomfortable situation–selling–and also help the company avoid the loss of a major account."

The bald manager raised his hand. "But what if Spike had insisted on talking to the customer and giving them his opinion?"

"Gil would have to tell Spike that he was no longer assigned to the account. The situation would be very sensitive with both the customer and Spike. However, Spike's thinking was misguided and Gil couldn't allow him to make decisions for his customer.

"Fortunately, in real life, Spike made a rational decision. He requested a transfer. It left a delicate sales problem for Gil to handle but the "Bread & Butter" account was saved."

Case 7

The Restroom

Background: You are still Gilbert Smith, Chief Product Manager. Every year, you and your Product Managers conduct a training program for your new representatives–people who have been recruited directly out of the universities. The program includes technical and skill training. After the first three months, the trainees start making customer calls with Account Representatives. By that time, they have been trained in customer relations and company standards for ethics and business practices. They know the importance of personal conduct to the success of the company.

You make great efforts to select the best people you can, the cream of the graduating classes. Their success will reflect on you. The company's success depends on their performance.

Today: You lead the last session on the last day of the first three months. It started off with a formal talk and ended with an informal question-and-answer session. By that time, you felt you knew the participants quite well. There are only four people in the class.

When you were finished, the trainees began filling out an evaluation form on your session. You left the conference room for your office. You then went to the restroom to occupy a stall. While there, you hear two trainees come in. You recognize their voices. They talk very positively about your session.

Then, Trainee A says, "Yeah, but isn't the guy a geek? Those glasses and that stupid grin. And you have to pretend you're buying everything he says."

Trainee B responds by laughing, "He's a nerd of the first kind. That bald head and fancy tie."

"I hope it isn't contagious," said Trainee A.

Both men have been outstanding in the classroom. They don't know that you have overheard them.

What Phase are you in? What do you do?

*   *   *   *   *   *   *

"I'd call out to 'em," said Angus. "I'd tell 'em they're bloomin' idiots."

"I'd tell them to come to my office," said the redhead, "then I'd go into a Phase 3 with them. I'd let them know I was concerned about how stupid they were to be talking like that in the company restroom."

"I don't know too much about what goes on in mens' restrooms," said Maria, as the class guffawed, "but I think it's more serious than Phase 3. I think we're in Phase 4 and maybe even in a verbal Phase 5. I'd tell them that if they were ever that foolish in the future that they'd be out the door. After all, if they did that at a customer location, they could threaten our business there–millions of dollars lost over childish behavior. We might have to lay workers off."

The bearded supervisor, a burly six footer, said, "I think I'd invite them to an informal meeting behind the barn to test what kind of nerd I was. But I agree with Maria, I think I'd put them on probation."

"Do you think you would ever catch them again?" asked Ed.

"They don't seem that dumb," said the redhead.

"And if you didn't catch them again, would you feel comfortable that they had learned their lesson? That they had stopped talking where they could be overheard? That they had sound judgment?"

The class looked around at each other. "Maybe, maybe not," said one fellow, who seemed to be expressing the view of the group.

"So they would pass whatever warning level you gave them," said Ed. "You wouldn't know if they were really changing their behavior, or if it only changed when they could be observed by management."

Again the class members looked around the room.

"You wouldn't fire them right now, would you?" asked the redhead.

The class fell silent as they reflected on the situation. Then heads began to nod.

"I guess I would," said Angus very quietly. "The company is paying for the cream."

Ed saw most of the class nodding. "You've come a long way," he said.

This time it was Maria who asked, "What actually happened?"

"Gilbert Smith decided not to confront the trainees from the stall. It was tempting but he wanted to think carefully about what he would say. The careers of the two trainees and the risk to the company were both important.

"That night, Gilbert called the two Product Managers that the two trainees were to work for. He told them his plan and asked for their comment.

"The next work day, a Monday, he called the two Product Managers and the two trainees into his office. He asked the trainees if they thought his session had been helpful to them. They immediately responded.

"Trainee A said, 'It was valuable. It put into perspective everything we've learned. You added a few things that tied it all together'.

"Trainee B said, 'It made us feel positive about working for this company'.

"Their easy, positive manner reminded the three managers of the favorable qualities they had seen in hiring the two trainees.

"Gilbert then asked his last question, 'Do you think I'm a nerd?'

"Their faces fell. They looked at each other and then at the managers. Guilt was written on their faces.

"Trainee A responded, 'Not really, sir'.

"The three managers looked at each other and nodded in agreement that a critical point had been verified.

"Gilbert leaned forward, his hands folded on his desk. 'I want you to know,' he said, 'that I would never fire someone because they thought ill of me. You obviously didn't know I was in a stall and overheard your conversation. That was careless of you. Some people would even call it stupid. It didn't reflect good judgment. It's certainly nothing we could risk happening with a customer. On that basis, you should go somewhere else to work.'

"Trainee A said, 'But, sir, I take full responsibility for getting us into that conversation. I was just joking around. It was the end of a long day. Trainee B just rode along with the joke.'

"Gilbert looked straight into Trainee A's eyes. 'You're to be commended on attempting to shoulder the responsibility. On the other hand, you've given yourself an excuse. 'You were only joking. It was the end of a long day'. In our line of work, we have lots of long days. We accept the fact that people make mistakes.'

"Trainee A said, 'Yes, sir. I made a mistake.'

"Gilbert responded, 'You made a mistake and then you compounded it by offering a lame excuse. I hope that you'll learn from this. Other companies may accept that kind of behavior. We don't.'

"Gilbert stood up and offered each of them his hand. 'You're both smart enough to be very successful. You'll do best if you start over somewhere else.'"

Ed had finished the story and looked at the class with his eyebrows raised, as if to ask, "Well?"

No one in the class asked what had happened to all of the Phases. By now, they realized that in selecting a course of action, you just needed to be mindful of what Phase you were in. And it must be consistent with good decision making. Knowing the Phase you are in helps determine your actions.

"I'll be damned," said Angus, "When I first heard about all these Phases, I thought it would take forever to fire someone."

The class nodded in agreement.

The bearded supervisor asked, "Isn't this a case where they could have considered transfer? The men had talent. They could have taken a job that wouldn't interface with customers."

"Almost true," said Ed. "That option was discussed among the managers. However, there were no suitable jobs within Gilbert Smith's organization that could offer career opportunities to satisfy the potential of the two trainees. In addition, the technical training they had received was minimal and not easily put to good use elsewhere in the company. Transferring them with such short tenure had risks. They might develop a bad attitude toward the company. They would probably not stay too long because they were talented people. It was best for everyone concerned to let them get a fresh start.

"Once that decision was reached, making it happen as quickly as possible–maintaining maximum respect possible for the employee–is the thing to do. You noticed that the way Gilbert handled it was respectful and polite to the trainees, and they accepted his decision without rancor–at least that's the way it was accepted in real life."

Ed saw that a number of class members were disturbed. "This is the most controversial case we have," he said. "Whether the decision was right or wrong depended heavily on the culture of the company. Many companies today would quickly turn their heads at such behavior–not even try to change it, but merely accept it as a part of today's expectations. This is not one of those companies. We have higher expectations."

Case 8

Executive Embezzlement?

Background: Sam joined a company as president of a new division. He was given total freedom in hiring his own staff but for the position of Vice President of Business Development, the corporate president recommended a company man, Chipper Hayes. Sam interviewed Chipper, hired him, and soon found Chipper to have different attitudes than others Sam was hiring. There was a looseness to everything Chipper did. Some called him devious. The suspicions caused problems in his dealings with members of the management team.

One day, Chipper approached Sam and said that the company owed him a lot of money for expense accounts he had not yet submitted from his previous position. Chipper guessed that it was close to $55,000, spanning many months. Sam was amazed and told him to submit his expense accounts to his previous manager. Chipper responded that the corporate president had said to settle it with Sam. Sam called the president for confirmation and then told Chipper to get his expense accounts in.

Weeks went by as Chipper gave one excuse after another for not submitting the expenses. He expressed an interest in negotiating an approximate amount in order to avoid the work of compiling all his records. Sam refused and finally gave him a deadline to either get them in or forget about them.

When submitted to Sam, the stack was formidable. Chipper casually apologized that some of the slips were missing but that he estimated them as closely and conservatively as he could on summary sheets. Chipper said, "I'm losing money on this, but it's worth it to get it all cleared up. I know that corporate accounting will approve. I've talked to them. I hope you'll send it over right away, because it's a lot of money they owe me."

Sam asked him, "But the receipts you do have here are all legitimate and actual?"

"Yes, sure," said Chipper, and then left the office.

Sam's Controller came by and saw the pile. "Bigger than I thought it would be," he said. "Want me to take it? You sure don't have time."

"Yes, I do," said Sam. Late that night he examined the mound. There were countless restaurant and hotel receipts, but most of them seemed to be reasonable–considering the amount of entertaining that Chipper did.

Then Sam noticed something unusual. For being so old, most of the receipts were not crumpled. He looked more closely and soon discovered that large groups of restaurant receipts were consecutively numbered even though the hand-written dates on them were shown as being days, weeks, or months apart. It was a fraud.

What Phase are you in? What are you going to do?

∗   ∗   ∗   ∗   ∗   ∗   ∗

This time, when Ed looked at the class, there were no raised hands. He said, "Good. Keep thinking."

"I'm afraid to say anything," said the bearded softie, "I'm always swinging too far one way or the other, but don't you have to fire him? You know, listen first to his excuses and then fire him."

"He's the corporate president's pet boy," said Maria. "He's been of value to the company before. You can't just fire him."

"I don't think," said the redhead, "that you want to have him around, always waiting for his next lie. He's already lost the confidence of the other managers, so this isn't the first thing he's done. Maybe the company president is just a wimp, maybe he knows of this kind of problem with Chipper and wants Sam to square him away."

"But it's the first time that Sam's caught him in a lie," said Angus. "That's all 'e has proof of."

"I'd talk to the company president," said Maria.

"Good," replied Ed, "That's actually what happened. Now, what would you say?"

"I'd ask him," said the bearded supervisor, "what he wanted me to do."

"No," said Angus, "The big mon would at least want to know what you proposed doing."

Maria shook her head. "If I was Sam, I'd tell the president that I didn't want Chipper in my organization anymore and that I was going to talk to him, listen to his excuses, and then fire him unless the president insisted that I not do that. And if the president wouldn't let me fire him, then I'd insist that the president take him back and decide what he wanted to do himself with good old Chipper."

"That's what happened," said Ed. "The president took him back, paid the $55,000, and life went on. It was no longer Sam's problem except that he now had an enemy in the corporate ranks."

"Sounds like Sam's the loser," said Angus.

"Quite likely," said Ed. "As long as the corporate president remains in office, Sam will probably be shielded from any political undermining by Chipper, but if the president leaves, Sam could become a target. Sometimes that's life in the executive suite. Some of it is messy. Perhaps if the corporate president had known the Five Phases he would have handled things differently with Chipper. Perhaps not. Maybe they have something on each other. Who knows?"

The balding man spoke up. "There's no guarantee that doing the right thing is risk-free," he said. Then looking at Ed, "Right?"

"Right," said Ed.

"How did it actually work out?" asked Angus.

Ed smiled. "Chipper hung around for almost two years and then left. He went into an unrelated business. Today, he's living in the Bahamas."

Case 9

Sexual Harassment?

Background: Three months ago you joined a small high-tech company as its president. Since the opening bell, the two founders of the company, the Vice President of Engineering and the Vice President of Advanced Development, have lobbied for you to fire the Vice President of Marketing and Sales. They blame him for slow sales, while he places the blame on poor product reliability, which the VP of Engineering is trying to improve.

According to Mr. Marketing's contract, if he is fired for any reason within the first three years–other than criminal–he will receive two years severance pay. He has been with the company 15 months.

You have steadfastly refused to fire Mr. Marketing, insisting that his previous record as a sales executive was outstanding and that he will be fairly tested when he has a reliable product to sell.

Some time passes. The National Service Manager tells you he has heard a rumor that Mr. Marketing was sexually pressuring one of the sales representatives in the Seattle Branch. You asked if there was any evidence. The answer was, 'No'. You asked if the Service Manager believed the rumors. The answer was a hesitation and then, 'I don't know'. You responded that you couldn't deal with rumors, and didn't want them perpetuated. You also said that you would listen to anything concrete.

Nevertheless, you decided to keep your ears open. Mr. Marketing is married with a large family.

The subject of sexual harassment is raised by others with similar results. The Seattle Office Manager called to tell you that he believed that Mr. Marketing was pressuring Sally and that Mr. Marketing always insisted that she pick him up at the airport when he came to town.

You asked, "Do you have any evidence of wrong doing?" The answer was, 'No'.

You asked, "Is she willing to speak up? Is she willing to make a complaint to either you or to the company?" The answer was, 'I don't think so'.

You asked, "Do you see any concrete way that this can be investigated without her stepping up to the plate?" The answer was again, 'No'.

Today: The Seattle Office Manager called. He said, "Sally is willing to make a complaint. She is willing to talk to you."

You talk to Sally. She tells you specifics that, if true, represent the worst kind of sexual harassment and job intimidation. She sounds sincere and coherent and afraid. You are inclined to believe her.

You know that to prove her case will require a lengthy investigation and considerable expense. You also realize that the accusations may be false. The company only has 300 employees and the internal politics of the past have been vicious.

What Phase are you in with Mr. Marketing? What do you do?

*   *   *   *   *   *   *

"You have to investigate it," said Maria insistently, "The company would be liable if you didn't."

"Correct," said Ed, noticing that Maria looked relieved.

"You're going to disrupt the whole organization if you start interviewing witnesses," said Angus. "It's a small company. The word will be out everywhere. While the investigation is going on, Mr. Marketing is probably going to lose his effectiveness."

"Right," said Ed.

"Sales are going to be 'urt," said Angus, "If the guy's innocent, the company is still going to be 'urt."

"Right," said Ed, "And what Phase are we in?"

"What's my relationship with Mr. Marketing?" asked the bearded one.

"Seems to me," said Maria, "that doesn't make any difference. The president has a responsibility he has to carry out. Although, I can see it might make a difference in how he says what he has to say, he still has to say it."

"And the Phase?" asked Ed again.

"Probably it's three, four, five, six," said Angus, "Don't sound like 'e needs any 'elp. 'e's probably 'elping 'imself plenty."

"Already guilty?" asked the redhead.

"No, but no surprise if 'e is. That's the way I'd be ready in the conversation."

"So, that's what you're going to do?" asked Ed, "You're going to meet with him? You're not going to do any other investigating first?"

The silence that followed was broken by Maria. "If you start an investigation, the cat is out of the bag, you'll spend a lot of money, and you probably won't find out much–not unless you set up a sting the next time the guy goes to Seattle. Then you may have a mess. Word will get out. He's got a wife. You could end up being sued if he's innocent. I'd vote to meet him head on. I'd start with Phase 3. I'd be ready to go right into Phase 4 and beyond. From here to eternity."

Ed saw that Maria had convinced the class. "And what do you say to Mr. Marketing?" he asked.

"I 'ope you're not playing around in the company sand box," said Angus. "Then I'd hear what 'e had to say."

"In a more polite way, that's what he was told," said Ed. "Here's the way it went–paraphrasing everything, of course."

President: "I've been told things I don't want to believe about your behavior. Are they true?"

Mr. Marketing: "What do you mean?"

President: "Sexual harassment and job intimidation."

Mr. Marketing had a guilty look before he even responded, "I'm not involved in anything like that. Those things are hard to prove. Who's making a complaint?"

President: "I can't expose the source. It's a woman. In the company. She's prepared to file a formal complaint if that's what it takes."

Mr. Marketing's face was frozen. "I didn't do anything wrong."

President: (Whose gut feeling told him of the guilt.):"Fair enough. She told me you did. She was very explicit. I'm in the unenviable position of having to respond to the accusation. You know that I can't let it drop. It seems that you have two choices: Number one: You can deny the charge, which forces me to conduct a thorough investigation. People will probably hear about it because several employees would have to give testimony. That might be uncomfortable for you, but we would try to conduct it as quietly as possible. If you're innocent, the truth will come out. Number two: You can decide that you are guilty of some indiscretions and resign. Or you can decide to resign for other reasons.

"The victim is not seeking recompense or retaliation. She just wants you gone."

Mr. Marketing sat in silence, probably thinking about what he was going to tell his wife. The guilt remained obvious–at least to the president.

President: "Well?"

Mr. Marketing: "You want an answer now?"

President: "Yes."

Mr. Marketing: After a long pause, "I'll resign."

President: "Okay. You might want to go to your office to write out your resignation, then bring it back. If I'm busy, interrupt me."

The VP of Marketing left and returned several minutes later with the handwritten resignation–the best kind in case he were to claim later that he was under undue pressure.

President: "I'm sorry that this all happened. It's best if you pack your things and leave before lunch. When you're ready, I'll check through the boxes. No one else has to be involved."

*   *   *

The bearded supervisor scratched his head, then softly asked, "Don't you have to be concerned about violence in situations like that? What if the guy gets physical?"

"Some companies insist that at least two people be there. Here, we leave it up to the individual manager's judgment. Sometimes the guilty party is less likely to confess if others are present."

The redhead asked, "Have you ever had someone go after you? Of course that's doubtful since you're six foot six."

"No, but twice I've been concerned about it. I told my secretary that if she didn't hear from me every ten minutes to ask another manager to step in. I've never seen anyone get violent who has gone through the Phases beginning at the right phase. But it could happen, especially in a case like this one where you jump in at Phase 3 and are prepared to go all the way in one conversation."

"And that was it with the VP of Marketing?" asked the redhead. "No big fight? No lawsuit? Just that straightforward?"

Ed nodded. "Fifteen minutes from start to finish–receiving the letter of resignation. It was another two hours to clear out. The president knew what Phase Mr. Marketing was in. It was too late to give him help or have a Dutch Uncle talk, or a 'serious' discussion. This was not a matter for probation, where it would expose other employees to his misconduct. It was time to say goodbye. The president wanted a resignation, so that's what he negotiated. He didn't want a major disruption to the company, which would have also been more troublesome to the employee and his wife.

"So I say again, 'What is best for the employee is usually best for the company and what is best for the company is usually best for the employee'. Once we accept that premise, solutions are much easier to find.

"Frank discussions can lead to quick resolutions. You don't have to be in a rage to fire someone. If you are, you're probably doing the wrong thing, or you've waited too long."

Chapter 7

Walking Away

At the luncheon that was held on the final day of class, Maria and Angus sat across the table from Ed. As the elected class president she had already made her brief speech, thanking her classmates and all of the instructors who had participated.

Ed was standing while making some last remarks. "Remember, just because a person reaches the pinnacle of management, it does not mean that the executive is comfortable in managing people. We would like to think that it does, but it doesn't. Look at Julius Redding's background–a barnstorming pilot, a brilliant aircraft designer. He had many management skills and many good people skills, but there were deficiencies. And Julius is not the exception. The top seats in many Fortune 500 firms are filled by experts from different disciplines.

"Some were financial wizards who never managed more than a few people but were cherished by the Board of Directors because they saved the company from financial disaster. Their appointment as CEO didn't suddenly make them effective managers of people. And today's environment is not that much different. The entrepreneurs starting technology companies that jump quickly to billions of dollars in sales don't have much time to study management. They are often only a few years out of school and what training they've had, if any, may be similar to that of Julius Redding.

"It doesn't mean that they are bad people. Because of their meteoric success, they just have not had the time to learn some of the management concepts that would help them. It's hard to send such people to class. Too bad this isn't in a book. They'd have time to read it.

"In our company, to make sure that all the executives are aware of these principles, every officer is invited to our sessions. That way, when you get back to your job, you can expect to have the understanding of your management."

Maria raised her hand. "What if our managers don't follow these guidelines, or even know about them?"

"That was a bigger concern a year ago before we held so many of these classes. But even then, we just advised everyone to go back to work, put this process into effect, and explain it to their manager. Get the Human Resources Department involved. They'll help everyone through the steps. They understand the Five Phases.

"However, in some companies, individuals have success-fully used the Five Phases without anyone else in the com-pany being aware of the process. They still get results."

After a stream of other questions, Ed sat down to a stand-ing applause.

"Lemon meringue pie," said Angus in an appreciative tone, as he finished his dessert.

Deciding to be straightforward, Maria placed her fork on her plate and looked at Ed. "I meant what I said in my speech. Everyone here admires your commitment to fairness . . ." She hesitated.

"But?" inquired Ed.

"But why do you take the time to personally teach?"

"Are you asking the question for everyone or for yourself?"

"No one in the class has mentioned it. They're glad you're here."

Ed looked at Angus and the others at their table who were watching with concerned expressions. "We'll be a better com-pany when our managers know the Five Phases. They'll be more likely to adopt it if they see I'm committed. If I were an author, I'd put this all in a book. Unfortunately, I'm not."

Maria boldly continued her questioning. "How long do you plan to keep teaching?"

"I'll finish the Five Phases in three more classes. By then I think they'll be part of our culture."

"So, in only 7 1/2 hours more of class time, your teaching career is over?" Maria asked the question as though she couldn't understand why her uncle and the Selection Committee had made such a big issue of it.

"There are other subjects," said Ed. He thought to himself, 'When some people hear that, they'll really be disturbed.'

"What course is next?" asked Angus.

Ed wondered if he would still be with the company. "No name yet," said Ed, "but it will likely be about leadership and productivity. To be a manager, you don't have to be a leader, but to be an outstanding manager, to be the most productive manager you can be, you have to be a leader. It's true at every level."

"You 'ave to 'ave a name," said Angus with his open smile.

"Maybe I'll call it '*The Joy of Managing—Leadership and Productivity*'," said Ed.

Angus nodded. "Joy. I like that."

"Or how do you like '*How to be a Management Leader— Not Just Another Bureaucrat*'?"

Angus grimaced. "I might enjoy a little '*Joy*' best," he said.

When the group had said its goodbyes, Maria lingered at the table with Ed. "You know why I was asking the questions?"

"I think so," he said.

"The answers don't help your personal battle."

"I know."

She tightened her mouth, nodded, then began walking away. She slowly came to a stop, and looked back over her shoulder with a wry smile on her face. "I hope you win the war." Then she added, "Maybe you should write that book."

*   *   *

And so the story ends, at least as far as we know here, for this is not a fable of procreation, but rather a chronicle of what managers can achieve if they are comfortable in themselves and in their mission. In that sense it is a collection of anecdotes which one friend might pass along to another. We save for a future day *The Theory of Uncomfortable Management.*

About the Author

The author's career is reflected in his no-nonsense approach and validates "Five-Phase Awareness" for organizations of every size. He has served as systems engineer, Human Resources VP, group executive, president, and member of the Board of Directors. He personally taught the Five Phases to over 1,000 managers and executives.

0-595-22142-4

www.ingramcontent.com/pod-product-compliance
Lightning Source LLC
Chambersburg PA
CBHW030850180526
45163CB00004B/1515

* 9 7 8 0 5 9 5 2 2 1 4 2 4 *